SIMPLE FIVE INGREDIENT CROCKPOT RECIPES

FOR BUSY PEOPLE

SAVING YOUR TIME, YOUR MONEY, AND YOUR HEALTH

BY: EMILY SIMMONS

Disclaimer:
The information presented in this book represents the views of the publisher as of the date of publication. The publisher reserves the rights to alter update their opinions based on new conditions. This report is for informational purposes only. The author and the publisher do not accept any responsibilities for any liabilities resulting from the use of this information. While every attempt has been made to verify the information provided here, the author and the publisher cannot assume any responsibility for errors, inaccuracies or omissions. Any similarities with people or facts are unintentional.

Table of Contents

Introduction 5
   Advantages of Using Your Slow Cooker 6
   Choosing a Slow Cooker 8
   Saving You Time 9
   Saving You Money 12
   Saving Your Health 14
   Let's Get Started 15
   Chicken Dishes 16
   Creamy Chicken and Mushroom Dinner 17
   Maple and Mustard Chicken 19
   Chicken and Baby Potato Dinner 21
   Instructions: 22
   Melting Mozzarella Chicken 23
   Chicken Fajitas 24
   Sweet and Sour Chicken 25
   Tangy Orange Chicken 26
   Sweet and Fiery Chicken 27
   Beef Dishes 28
   Simple Beef Ragu 29
   Brisket Pot-roast with Cranberry Sauce 31
   Slow Cooker "Lasagna" 33
   Beef and Vegetable Dinner 35
   Pork Dishes 37
   Sweet and Sticky Pork Ribs 38
   Pork Chops with Applesauce and Sweet Potatoes 39
   Sweet 'n Slow Pineapple Pork Chops 40
   Pulled Pork in Cola 41
   Pulled Pork Wraps 43
   Golden Butternut Soup 46
   Buttery Herby Baby Potatoes 48

Roast Vegetables 52
Creamy Potato Soup.. 53
Macaroni and Cheese 54
Sweet Pleasures 56
Breakfast Honeyed Pear Compote 57
Crustless Baked Cheesecake... 59
Stewed Apples with Custard 61
AppleBerry Dessert with Vanilla Ice-Cream......................... 62

Conclusion.. 64

Introduction

Hello, and welcome to this exciting new recipe book. I say "exciting" because you're going to save so much time that would otherwise be spent

in the kitchen. These super-easy recipes are going to free you up to get on and do other things while your meals slowly simmer away, becoming more tender and delicious with every passing hour.

You're also going to save money, because the recipes use simple ingredients- nothing fancy here- and there's little wastage. You'll also save on electricity when you use your slow cooker.

I also claim to save your health. Well, what I mean by this is that instead of buying greasy take away meals because you're pressed for time, you'll

be able to do some good wholesome home cooking using fresh, simple ingredients, without spending hours in the kitchen.

The recipes are also great because they all use a maximum of 5 ingredients, simplifying your shopping list, too. Many of the ingredients

can be kept in your store cupboard or freezer, making them even more convenient.

So, let's look at some of this in a bit more detail before getting into the recipes.

Advantages of Using Your Slow Cooker

A slow cooker (or Crockpot to use the common brand name) is something that most of us have, but few of us use to its full potential. It was probably given to us by a parent or auntie, used once or twice, then stored away with those other neglected kitchen appliances like electric can openers and coffee filter machines. It's time to dust it off and take it out of that forgotten cupboard!

One way of ensuring that you'll use it more is to clear a corner on the kitchen workspace where you can leave it out and plugged in. Having its own space will mean it's that much easier to quickly pop your ingredients in and switch it on. The inner dish is easily taken out and washed (no burned-on crusty bits), while the outer metal/ceramic part can be wiped down when you clean the countertops. You won't use it if you have to pack it away into the cupboard after every **time you use it.**

Cooking with your slow cooker means that you will have far fewer dishes to wash up as well. Most of the recipes just call for you to dump the 5 ingredients straight into the pot, but some may call for a bit of browning of the meat or onions first. This takes just a few minutes and can really make a difference to the flavors.

Another lovely thing about the slow cooker is that it's not just an appliance for winter. Although it makes wonderful hot soups and stews for the cold months, it is also nice to use in summer because it saves putting the oven on (which heats up the entire area even more.)

Summertime things to make in it would be, for example, a piece of pork

for pulled pork rolls or wraps, or a whole chicken all ready to debone and use in fresh summer salads.

Choosing a Slow Cooker

Well, let's not assume we all have a slow cooker gathering dust in a corner somewhere. Let's say you're in the market for one but don't know where to start.

Basically, Crock Pot is just a brand name for a certain make of slow cooker. There are many others out there on the market, so don't be confused by the name. They're essentially all similar: a simple kitchen appliance made up of an outer casing that contains a heating element, and an inner dish, often made of ceramic, to put the food into.

Be sure to choose the right size for your family. If you're a single person who lives alone, you don't want to be using, and washing, an enormous family-sized dish. However, if you want to double up on recipes so that you'll have handy leftovers, or want to cook roasts or whole chickens, then bear in mind that they won't fit into a small slow cooker. For just two people, a 3-4-quart cooker is big enough. For bigger families, a 6-quart cooker is recommended.

Crock pots with a rounded or oval shape are easier to clean, as are ones with a removable dish. You don't want to be washing the entire thing while trying to keep the electricals from getting wet.

Glass lids are nice as they're more durable than plastic ones, plus you can see what's going on inside without lifting the lid.

Well, I hope this helps when you go to choose your new cooker!

Saving You Time

It may seem strange that something that takes nine hours to cook a meal can save you time, but in reality it does. You spend just a few minutes prepping the ingredients. You then put them all into the cooker, switch it on, and then forget all about it. You don't need to turn the food, stir it, or watch it in any way. This frees you up to get on with other things.

A time-saving tip is to double the recipe so that half can be kept for another day, or frozen. A popular idea is to prepare the meals in Ziploc (resealable) bags, putting in the raw meat, the prepared vegetables, the sauce ingredients, and the herbs and spices, then freezing it all together.

This meal-in-one mixture can then be quickly defrosted in the microwave when you're ready to cook, dumped straight into the crockpot, and that's it. Some people prepare several of these bags on the weekend and freeze them for the coming weeks.

Another good idea if you're going to have a busy time the next day, is to prepare everything the night before (peel and chop the vegetables etc.) put them into the slow cooker dish, cover it, and put it in the fridge overnight. In the morning you can just take it out, put the meal into the cooker case and switch it on. When you come home after your busy day dinner will be ready and waiting for you.

The only items you'll have to wash afterwards will probably be a chopping board, knife, the slow cooker bowl itself, and your plate and cutlery. No more scrubbing away at dirty pots and pans! The inner slow cooker dish is very easy to wash if you fill it with hot soapy water after dinner. Let it soak for a few minutes, then everything wipes away easily. You can then dry it and put it straight back into the outer case, ready to use for the next meal.

Remember not to overfill the slow cooker bowl. Fill it about halfway, or to a maximum of three quarters full. Also, you need less liquid than with conventional cooking, as there's very little evaporation. Try not to keep lifting the lid to check the food all the time, as heat will be lost this way. It will not catch and burn if there was liquid put in at the beginning.

An advantage as well is that tougher, cheaper, and more flavorful cuts of meat such as chick or brisket can be used. The long, slow cooking

process dissolves all the tough connective tissue, leaving you with moist, tender meat and a rich, delicious gravy or sauce. The tougher meat and hard vegetables like carrots and parsnips are better placed at the bottom

of the dish (nearer the heat sauce and under the liquid), while more delicate vegetables like broccoli or mushrooms can be put on top to steam.

What's great is that most cookers automatically switch off "HI" or "LOW" mode once the cooking time has finished, and switch onto "WARM." In this way your food won't get overcooked, or get cold while waiting for you.

You can put your dinner on after 10 minutes of prep in the morning before you go to work, and come home to the aromas of lunch or dinner

all ready and waiting for you. Or you can make a lovely dessert without even switching the oven on!

To save yourself time with shopping, try to make out a weekly menu based on the recipes, and make a shopping list based on this. This will

mean that you will know ahead of time what's for dinner, and will be confident that you have all the ingredients you'll need for the recipes.

There'll also be less wastage of fresh ingredients, as every item you buy

will be used up by the end of the week.See I told you I'd save you money!)
Which leads to the next paragraph…

Saving You Money

I don't make this claim lightly because I know that I too get annoyed by every second book claiming to make me a millionaire overnight or save me hundreds of dollars if I'll spend a thousand on their products first. Using this book won't make you rich, but it will save you some precious dollars on your grocery budget to be able to use for other things. Our grocery budgets are probably the one expense we have that isn't fixed, and it is the one area that is easiest to cut down on.

Home cooked meals are usually always more economical than buying ready-made foods from the frozen section of the supermarket, or dining out at a restaurant. Remember, restaurants and fast-food diners have to cover all their business overhead costs (rent, electricity, staff, cleaning chemicals etc.) Yes, they do get bulk discounts, but so can you if you shop wisely and buy special offers in bulk.

As mentioned before, cheaper cuts of meat can be used in the slow cooker, which will save you plenty without having to resort to horrible processed meats.

You may be wondering if using the slow cooker really will save you electricity when compared to an oven, seeing as it's on for such a long time.
Without going into detail on all the figures, most tests seem to indicate that it takes one third the amount of energy to cook a meal in the slow cooker as opposed to the oven. That's assuming your stew or whatever will be in the oven for one hour and in the crock pot for eight. The crockpot uses just a bit more power than a conventional light bulb. So you should save on your electricity bill as well as your grocery one.

Saving Your Health

I've made this claim based on the fact that the recipes in this book rely largely on a balance of fresh protein sources, fresh or frozen vegetables,

and fresh or dried herbs and spices. There is a selection of vegetarian meals as well.

We all know that home-cooked meals are better for us than greasy take-aways or pizzas made with refined flour. I've tried to avoid processed

foods and artificial colorants and flavorings, and stuck to basic meats, veg, herbs, and spices in this book. Even the desserts have very little

sugar and refined goods in them, and rely mainly on fruits of wholesome dairy products.

There is less fat in these meals, as you aren't frying anything, and all visible fat is trimmed from the meat before cooking.

You can see exactly what goes into your food, and can tailor the meals to suit your family members. Because there aren't long lists of ingredients,

you can quickly read them and make any changes you need to for your family. For example, if someone in your family can't eat mushrooms and

cream of mushroom soup is called for, you can substitute cream of chicken soup.

Let's Get Started

In this book I've given you a selection of meal-in-one recipes ranging from chicken, to beef, to pork, and even some vegetarian meals for "meat free Mondays."
There are a few sweet treats to end off with too.

So, I hope you enjoy making these recipes as much as I have enjoyed putting them together for you. Happy slow-cooking!

Chicken Dishes

Always popular and so versatile, chicken is something that most people eat. Children enjoy its mild flavors too. Here's a sampling of chicken dishes, some of which are smooth and creamy, others that are Asian inspired with sweet/sour flavors, and a couple of family-friendly ones with potatoes and vegetables.

Remember to trim any visible fat off before starting, and you can even remove the skin if you prefer. Where the breast meat is used, it will stay moist and succulent, and will not dry out like it tends to in the oven.

Creamy Chicken and Mushroom Dinner

Let this dish bubble away quietly while you get on with more important matters. The small quantity of cream really adds a rich silkiness to the

sauce. You can substitute it with coconut cream if you like, for a slightly different flavor. You may also use long-life cream in a box if you want to.

I like to keep a few of these in my pantry, then I know I always have cream on hand for recipes like this.

Try to get canned soup with no colorings and artificial additives- there are brands available like this.

Ingredients:
700g boneless, skinless chicken breasts
250g button mushrooms, wiped and sliced
1 can of cream of mushroom soup
Small handful parsley, chopped
125ml cream

Instructions:
Spray the slow cooker dish with non-stick cooking spray.
Lay the chicken in the base of your slow cooker.
Scatter the mushrooms over the top.
Mix the soup, parsley, and cream together in a small bowl, then pour this over the chicken.
Cook on HIGH for 4 hours or LOW for 6 hours.
Check seasoning.
Serve on brown rice or on pasta with a salad.

Serves 4

Maple and Mustard Chicken

Substitute honey if you don't have maple syrup, then rename this "Honey Mustard Chicken." Either way, it's yummy.

You may leave the chicken breasts whole or slice them smaller. Again, if you have a box of long-life cream on the shelf, and frozen chicken in the freezer, you'll have everything on hand for an easy dinner.

Ingredients:
6 chicken breast fillets
60ml maple syrup
80ml whole grain mustard
250ml cream
1 teaspoon paprika

Instructions:

Spray the slow cooker dish with non-stick cooking spray.
Put the chicken into the slow cooker.
Using a separate bowl, whisk together the maple syrup, mustard, cream and paprika, and some seasoning.
Cover, and cook on HIGH for about 3 hours.
Serve on steamed rice with vegetables.

Serves 6

Chicken and Baby Potato Dinner

The potatoes soak up the delicious chicken flavors and end up creamy and soft. Feel free to use cream of mushroom or cream of vegetable soup if you prefer.
You may cube the chicken breasts or leave them whole.

Ingredients:
About 2 dozen baby potatoes, halved
700g skinless and boneless chicken breasts
2 cans cream of chicken soup
1 teaspoon dried thyme
1 teaspoon dried garlic flakes

Instructions:
Spray the slow cooker dish with non-stick cooking spray, or grease with butter.
Lay the potato halves in the bottom of the slow cooker.
Spread the chicken over the top.
In a medium-sized bowl, mix the soup, thyme, and garlic, and pour this over the chicken.
Cook on HIGH for 4 hours or LOW for 7 hours.
Check seasoning.
Serve in warmed bowls sprinkled with a garnish of fresh thyme.

Serves 4

Melting Mozzarella Chicken

This dish has flavors that are reminiscent of pizza. Use salami in place of bacon for a variation that is just as good.

Ingredients:
6 chicken breast fillets, flattened slightly with a meat mallet
30 ml tomato paste
1 teaspoon dried oregano
6 slices bacon
6 big slices mozzarella cheese

Instructions:
Season each chicken fillet with some salt and pepper, then spread with tomato paste.
Sprinkle each one with a little oregano.

Grease the bottom of the slow cooker with a little olive oil.
Place the chicken carefully on the bottom of the slow-cooker, then cover and cook on

HIGH for 2 hours or LOW for 4 hours. There is no need to add any liquid.
When almost ready to serve, remove the chicken from the cooker and lay on **a baking sheet.**

Heat the grill, grill the bacon and put a slice onto each chicken piece. Lastly, top with mozzarella.

Grill until the cheese is just melted, then serve at once, spooning the juices left in the cooker over it.
Serve with baked potatoes and a salad.

Serves 4

Chicken Fajitas

Everyone can have fun assembling their own fajitas. Provide plenty of toppings and you'll have a feast with minimal effort. Buy ready-made fajita spice if you can find it, or make your own.
Homemade stock is always best, but if you don't have any choose a low-sodium brand if you can.

For extra flavor, the strips of pepper and onion can be stir-fried in a little oil until softened before putting them into the slow cooker, but this is not essential.

Ingredients:
1 each red, yellow, and green bell peppers, cut into strips
1 onion, peeled and cut into strips
3 teaspoons fajita spice (made with ½ teaspoon each chili powder, paprika, cumin, garlic powder, onion powder, chili flakes)
600g chicken breast fillets, cut into strips
½ cup strong chicken stock

Instructions:
Spray the slow cooker dish with non-stick cooking spray.
Place the peppers and onion at the bottom of the slow cooker.
Put chicken strips on top, and sprinkle with spice.
Pour the stock over, and season well.
Cover and cook on LOW for about 5 hours, or HIGH for about 3 hours.
Leave it to cool slightly, then pull the chicken apart with 2 forks.
Serve inside flour tortillas along with fillings of your choice, such as grated cheddar cheese, shredded lettuce, salsa, mashed avocado and sour cream.

Sweet and Sour Chicken

Ever-popular Asian flavors make a super-easy meal. Serve with noodles if you prefer, and make a side of frozen stir-fry vegetables for an easy and healthy complete dish.

Ingredients:
5 chicken breast fillets, cut into strips
1 small can pineapple pieces, drained
1 each green and red pepper, thinly sliced
1 bunch spring onions, chopped
½ bottle sweet and sour sauce

Instructions:
Spray the slow cooker dish with non-stick cooking spray.
Put the peppers and onions on the base of the slow cooker.
Put the chicken on top.
Add the pineapple, and lastly, top with the sweet and sour sauce.
Cover, and cook on HIGH for 3 hours or LOW for 5.
Serve on rice or noodles with a stir-fry of vegetables.

Serves 4

Tangy Orange Chicken

Don't be put off by the marmalade in this recipe. Give it a try and you'll see that it imparts a lovely fresh orange flavor and provides some sweetness to compliment the chicken and the carrots.

Ingredients:
4 chicken breast fillets, cubed
300g frozen baby carrots
60ml sweet orange marmalade
175ml BBQ sauce of your choice
30ml soy sauce

Instructions:
Spray the slow cooker dish with non-stick cooking spray.
Place the chicken and carrots in the bottom of the slow cooker, and season well with salt and pepper.
In a small bowl, mix the marmalade, BBQ sauce, and soy sauce together.
Pour over the chicken.
Cover and cook on HIGH for 4 hours.
Serve with steamed white rice and green beans.

Serves 4

Sweet and Fiery Chicken

This is a spin on the Panda-Express favorite.

Ingredients:
5 chicken breast fillets, cut into small cubes
1 cup hot sweet chili sauce
1 can pineapple chunks (about 410g), drained but 125ml juice reserved
1 yellow and 1 red bell pepper, chopped
1 small onion, finely chopped

Instructions:
Spray the slow cooker dish with non-stick cooking spray.
Put the chicken, onion, and peppers into the crockpot.
Pour the pineapple juice over the top.
Cover and cook on HIGH for 3 hours.
Pour in the hot sweet chili sauce and cook for another 30 min on HIGH.
If the juices are too thin, thicken with a little cornstarch mixed with water.
Serve on steamed white rice.

Serves 4

Beef Dishes

Come home to a deliciously rich beef ragu, or a comforting pot roast like Grandma used to make. Did you know that you can even make lasagna in the slow cooker? Try these yummy recipes and you'll come back for more.

Cooking your beef cuts in the slow cooker will result in succulent, tender meat that just falls off the bone. Even the chewiest cuts of meat will be

softened by the combination of slow, gentle cooking and added liquid to dissolve the tough collagen fibers.

Using the bones will result in even more flavor in the sauce, and these can always be removed prior to serving.

Cuts of beef such as shin, chuck, brisket, oxtail, and beef cheek are perfect for slow cooking at low temperatures. The addition of liquids such as wine or balsamic vinegar helps to soften the meat too.

Simple Beef Ragu

You may use boneless beef ribs for a shorter cooking time, but the bones do impart a wonderful flavor to the dish.

Ingredients:
1.5kg beef short ribs, cut into short pieces or deboned by your butcher
2 cloves garlic, peeled and crushed
4 carrots, peeled and diced
1 can (about 410g) Italian tomatoes, with Italian herbs
1 cup red wine

Instructions:

Season the beef well with salt and pepper, and put it into your slow cooker.

Add the garlic, carrots, tomatoes and wine.

Cover and cook on HIGH for 7 hours or LOW for 10 hours.

Meat should be tender and falling off the bone.

Taste and check seasoning. Add extra herbs such as basil if you feel they are needed.

Cool slightly then remove bones. If the sauce is too runny, it can be strained off and reduced in a small saucepan, but this shouldn't be necessary.

Serve on pasta or mashed potato, garnished with fresh basil leaves.

Serves 4

Brisket Pot-roast with Cranberry Sauce

A wholesome roast that will impress anybody. They'll think you've spent hours in the kitchen preparing this sumptuous meal! Use the leftover

beef for sandwiches or wraps.
If you want to cut down on fat, prepare this dish the day before, then put

it into the fridge. Once it's cold any extra fat will have hardened on top and can be removed and discarded.

Ingredients:

1 whole beef brisket, about 1 ½ kg
1 big onion, chopped
1 can (about 400g) cranberry sauce
15ml Dijon mustard
250ml strong beef stock

Instructions:
Place brisket in your slow cooker.
Top with the onion.
Mix the cranberry sauce, mustard, and stock, and pour into the cooker.
Cover and cook on LOW about 10 hours or until meat is falling apart.
Remove the meat and carve it into thin slices.
You may reduce the cooking juices and serve them poured over the meat as a gravy, or thicken them first with a little cornstarch mixed to a slurry with a bit of water. (About a dessertspoon of each.)
Serve with mashed potatoes and green vegetables.

Serves 6

Slow Cooker "Lasagna"

Whoever would have thought you can make lasagna in the crockpot! Use whatever flavor of ravioli you prefer- the beef one is merely a suggestion.

Chicken ravioli would work well too.
You may reduce the quantity of cheese if you like.

Ingredients:

2 packages ready-made beef ravioli, thawed if frozen
1 jar tomato pasta sauce (about 500g)
1 jar readymade cheese sauce (about 250g)
500ml grated mozzarella cheese
1 teaspoon dried oregano

Instructions:

First, spray the slow cooker dish with non-stick cooking spray.
Starting with the pasta sauce, make layers in the slow cooker dish.
Layer the sauce, then the ravioli, then some cheese sauce, and lastly mozzarella and a sprinkling of oregano.
Continue layering until all your ingredients are used up.
Lastly, sprinkle the top with some oregano.
Cover and cook on HIGH for 3 hours.
Serve with a fresh salad.

Serves 4

Beef and Vegetable Dinner

This is so useful- a complete meal in one. It is correct that there is so much liquid because the rice absorbs it as it cooks. If you feel that

towards the end of cooking time it's becoming too dry, then add a little more stock. Don't stir the dish at any time of the rice will become stodgy.
Add a big pinch of dried rosemary for extra flavor if you like.

Ingredients:
300g sliced button mushrooms
3 carrots, peeled and cut into rings
170g brown rice
500g beef rump, cubed
1 ¼ liters strong hot beef stock

Instructions:
Put the mushrooms, carrot rings, and rice into the slow cooker and mix together.
Put the meat on top.
Pour the stock over everything.
Put the lid on and cook on LOW for about 8 hours.
When done, check seasoning.
Serve in warmed bowls with a sprig of fresh rosemary to garnish.
Serves 4

Pork Dishes

Pork is ideal for making in the slow cooker, as it becomes wonderfully tender, and sweet and absorbs the flavors of the sauce beautifully.

"Pulled pork" has become quite trendy, especially when served in wraps or tortillas. Here you'll find recipes for pork with traditional apple, which

always combine so well together, and also with pineapple for a Chinese twist, and even pork cooked in cola for sweetness and tenderness.

Sweet and Sticky Pork Ribs

Enjoy eating these delicious sticky morsels with your fingers. Be sure not to use diet cola, as the results will not be the same.

Ingredients:
About 1 ½ kg pork ribs, cut into pieces by your butcher
500ml BBQ sauce
250ml cola
60ml apple juice
Salt and pepper

Instructions:
Season the ribs with salt and pepper, then put into the slow cooker.
In a small bowl, mix the BBQ sauce, cola, and apple juice.
Pour this over the ribs.
Cover and cook on HI for about 5 hours, or LOW for about 8 hours, until the meat is falling off the bone.
Serve with rice.

Serves 4

Pork Chops with Applesauce and Sweet Potatoes

Sweet and succulent, these pork chops are a sure winner.

Ingredients:
400g sweetened applesauce
3 big sweet potatoes peeled and diced
6 pork loin chops, fat and rind removed
Salt and pepper
15ml honey

Instructions:
Spray the slow cooker dish with non-stick cooking spray.
First put the applesauce into the bottom of the slow cooker.
Then layer the sweet potatoes on top, seasoning them well.
Lastly, put in the pork chops, and seasoning and drizzle with the honey.
Cover, and cook on LOW for about 7 hours until everything has softened.

Serves 6

Sweet 'n Slow Pineapple Pork Chops

Ingredients:
1 can (about 220g) crushed pineapple, do not drain
250ml bottled BBQ sauce
I large onion, finely chopped
1 fresh red chili, seeded and finely chopped
4 pork loin chops, fat removed

Instructions:
Spray the slow cooker dish with non-stick cooking spray.
Mix together the pineapple, BBQ sauce, onion, and chili in a bowl.
Put half of this mixture into the slow cooker.
Place the chops on top, then top with the rest of the sauce.
Cover and cook on HIGH for about 3-4 hours.
Serve with mashed potatoes and green beans or peas.

Serves 4

Pulled Pork in Cola

The cola adds a sweet, spicy flavor, as well as tenderizes the meat. Don't use diet cola, as in this case the sugar/ corn syrup is necessary.

You can also try this with ginger ale. If you do, try adding a teaspoon of grated fresh ginger to really bring out that gorgeous ginger flavor.

This recipe has just 4 ingredients, but that's all that are needed to let the taste of the meat shine through.

Ingredients:

1 ½ kg pork loin roast, fat and skin removed
Salt and pepper
350ml cola
About 250ml bottled BBQ sauce

Instructions:
Spray the slow cooker dish with non-stick cooking spray.

Rub the pork all over with seasoning, then place in the slow cooker.
Pour the cola around the meat.

Cook on LOW for around 12 hours until pork is falling apart.
Remove from the liquid and pull apart with 2 forks.

The liquid in the cooker can be placed in a saucepan on the stove and reduced.
The meat is then mixed with this sauce.

Add some BBQ sauce for flavor if you like.
Serve the meat and sauce in soft fresh bread rolls with coleslaw on the side, or use it in tortilla wraps.

Pulled Pork Wraps

Ingredients:
4 slices streaky bacon
1 Boston butt roast
4 cloves garlic
1 jar sweetened applesauce
8 flour tortillas

Instructions:
Spray the slow cooker dish with non-stick cooking spray.
Lay the bacon on the bottom of the slow cooker to form a base for the roast.
Rub the roast well with salt and pepper.
Make small slits in the meat with a sharp knife, and insert the garlic cloves.
Put the meat into the cooker, and cover. (No liquid is added.)
Cook for 12-14 hours on LOW until the meat is falling apart.
Remove the meat and shred it, using 2 forks to pull it apart.
Discard the bacon or shred it in with the meat.

Put the meat back into the juices in the cooker as you go, to moisten it. When ready to serve, spread each tortilla with applesauce, then fill with pork before folding into pockets.

Serve with coleslaw.

Serves 4

Vegetarian Dishes

Even if you're not vegetarian, you'll enjoy using these recipes for easy lunches, or as side dishes for barbeques. There are two different soups here, and even a comforting pasta classic.

Golden Butternut Soup

This bright and sunny soup is always a hit. Add a cinnamon stick while cooking it if you like its sweet and aromatic flavor.

Ingredients:
1 onion, chopped
3 medium carrots, peeled and chopped
1 large butternut squash, peeled, seeded and cubed
1 big sweet potato, peeled and chopped
500ml strong chicken stock

Instructions:
Put the prepared vegetables into the slow cooker.
Pour the stock over.
Cover and cook on HIGH for 3 hours, or LOW for 4 hours.
When everything has softened, blend to a smooth puree.
If the soup is too thick, add a little more of the hot stock or some milk.
Serve with a swirl of cream and a sprinkle of ground cinnamon.

Serves about 6

Buttery Herby Baby Potatoes

These are a useful side dish for a barbeque or meat dish. You can also have them as a complete meal, perhaps with a little bacon or grated cheese on top.

Ingredients:
1kg baby potatoes, halved
60ml butter, melted
2 cloves garlic, crushed
Handful of fresh mixed herbs, such as parsley, thyme, rosemary
Bunch of spring onions, green parts included, finely chopped

Instructions:
Spray the slow cooker dish with non-stick cooking spray.
Using a small bowl, mix the butter, garlic, herbs and onions.
Place the potatoes in the slow cooker, and pour the butter mix over.
Cover and cook on HIGH for about 3 hours, or low for about 6 hours, until the potatoes are very soft.
Serve hot.

Moreish Mashed Potatoes

These soft and creamy mashed potatoes are a little different to those usually made with milk.

Ingredients:
1kg potatoes, peeled and cut into quarters
½ cup strong chicken stock
125g cream cheese
30ml snipped fresh chives
30ml butter

Instructions:

Put the potatoes into the slow cooker and cover with salted water.
Cover and cook on HI for about 3 hours or LOW for about 6 hours.

When the potatoes are soft, drain them then put them back in the cooker.
Add the stock, cream cheese, chives and butter.

Season with salt and pepper.
Mash well until very smooth, adding more stock if necessary.
Garnish with a few more chives before serving hot.

Serves 4

Roast Vegetables

Use a selection of whatever vegetables you have. Mushrooms, pumpkin, potatoes, green beans, or onion will all work well together.

Ingredients:
1 red and 1 yellow bell pepper, cut in big chunks
1 large sweet potato, peeled and cubed
4 small baby marrows, cut into thirds
1 butternut, cut up coarsely
30ml olive oil

Instructions:
Place the vegetables into the slow cooker.
Pour in the oil and some seasonings of your choice (salt, pepper, oregano, garlic.)
Mix everything together with your hands, ensuring all the vegetables are coated in oil and seasoning.
Cover and cook on HIGH for about 3-4 hours, or LOW for about 6 hours.

Serves 4

Creamy Potato Soup

This simple soup is rich, filling, and comforting on a cold winter's day.

Ingredients:
850g potatoes, peeled and coarsely grated
1 can (about 410g) cream of mushroom or chicken soup
500ml chicken stock
1 large onion, peeled and finely diced
250ml fresh cream

Instructions:
Put the potatoes, canned soup, stock, and onion into the slow cooker.
Cook on LOW for 5-7 hours.
Pour in the cream and cook for another half hour on LOW, to heat the cream
Check seasoning, and add salt and pepper if needed.
Garnish with snipped chives or crisp bacon bits if you like.

Serves 4-6

Macaroni and Cheese

Ingredients:
500g macaroni pasta, raw
450g cheddar cheese, grated
1 liter milk
15ml butter
10ml onion powder

Instructions:

Spray the slow cooker dish with non-stick cooking spray, or grease it with extra butter.
Put everything into the slow cooker.
Mix together well.
Cook on HIGH for 2 hours or on LOW for 3 hours.

Serves 4-6

Sweet Pleasures

These fruity recipes are easy, healthy, and so convenient. The stewed desserts can be used for breakfast, too, along with plain yoghurt and

muesli. Serve them with cream, ice-cream, or custard for a dessert your whole family will love, or bake a cheesecake without using the oven, for a special treat.

The stewed fruits can be kept in the fridge for about a week and can even be pureed and used as baby food or as a sauce for pork.

Breakfast Honeyed Pear Compote

Substitute apples for the pears, if you like, or try a combination of apples, pears, and peaches.
Your baby will love this pureed, only leave the ginger out.

Ingredients:
2kg pears, peeled, cored, and diced
30ml honey
15ml grated fresh ginger
60ml apple juice

Instructions:
Spray the slow cooker dish with non-stick cooking spray.
Put the prepared pears into the crockpot.
Drizzle with the honey.
Mix the apple juice with the ginger and pour over the fruit.
Cover and cook on HIGH for 2 hours or LOW for 4 hours or until pears are soft.
Cool and refrigerate.

Serve with scoops of full cream plain yoghurt, with an extra drizzle of honey, or with granola.

Crustless Baked Cheesecake

Ingredients:
750g low fat cream cheese, softened
160ml white sugar
15ml cake flour
2 big eggs
5ml vanilla essence

Instructions:
Use an 18cm diameter spring form pan, and a 6 quart slow cooker or larger, with a rack.
Spray the pan with non-stick cooking spray.
Put the cream cheese in a mixer, and beat until smooth.
Add the sugar, flour, eggs, and vanilla, and beat together well.
Pour into the pan.
Place the rack in the slow cooker, along with 250ml hot water.
The water should be below the level of the rack so it does not touch the spring form pan.

Place the pan on the rack and put a clean dish towel over the top

where the slow cooker's lid goes. (This stops the condensing water from dripping onto your cheesecake.)
Put the lid on.

Cook on HIGH and cook for 2 hours, or until the cheesecake is set and slightly wobbly in the middle.

Turn the cooker off, but leave the cheesecake inside for another hour to firm up.

Cool, and then refrigerate for at least 8 hours before removing outer ring of the pan.

Serve sliced and garnished with berries and cream, or with a caramel sauce.

Makes 1 cheesecake

Stewed Apples with Custard

This delightful vintage dessert is bound to please the whole family. You can even puree the apples for baby food.

Ingredients:
1.5kg apples, peeled, cored, and cubed
60ml sugar or honey
60ml water or apple juice
2 cinnamon sticks
500ml ready-made custard or vanilla ice-cream

Instructions:
Spray the slow cooker with non-stick cooking spray.
Place the cinnamon sticks on the bottom, then top with the apples.
Pour the water or apple juice over the top, then sprinkle with the sugar.
Cover and cook on HIGH for about 2 hours, or LOW for about 4 hours, or until the apples are soft.
Remove the cinnamon sticks and allow to cool.
Serve warm or at room temperature with custard.

Serves 4

AppleBerry Dessert with Vanilla Ice-Cream

Serve in bowls for a simple family pudding, or in beautiful glasses with a rounded scoop of the best vanilla ice-cream for a sophisticated dinner party.

Ingredients:
1kg apples, peeled, cored, and chopped
500g fresh or frozen berries, such as blackberries, youngberries, or strawberries
125ml white sugar
15ml lemon juice
Vanilla ice-cream to serve

Instructions:
Spray the slow cooker with non-stick cooking spray.
Put in the apples and berries.
Sprinkle with sugar and lemon juice.
Cook on LOW for about 4-5 hours, until the apples are soft.
Cool to room temperature and serve with the ice-cream.

Serves 4-6

Conclusion

I hope you'll come back to this little book again and again and that it will simplify your life. At the end of the day, I think we all want the best for our families in terms of time, health, and money, and hopefully these recipes will help to a small extent with that.

As you get more used to using your slow cooker, I'm sure you'll begin to adapt your favorite family recipes and use it even more. Even the children can be taught how to dump the prepared ingredients in, and switch on the timer.
Have fun!

www.ingramcontent.com/pod-product-compliance
Lightning Source LLC
LaVergne TN
LVHW020419070526
838199LV00055B/3671